Musical Theatre Classics

Performed by: Shannon Forsell, singer • Rick Walters, Sue Malmberg, pianists
Vocals recorded at the Chicago Recording Company, 12/95, Jeffrey Lane, engineer

ISBN 0-7935-6236-8

HAL•LEONARD®
CORPORATION

7777 W. BLUEMOUND RD. P.O. BOX 13819 MILWAUKEE, WI 53213

ABOUT THE SHOWS...

ANNIE GET YOUR GUN
Opened on Broadway: 5/16/46
Music & Lyrics: Irving Berlin
Book: Herbert & Dorothy Fields
Director: Josh Logan
Choreographer: Helen Tamiris

The story goes that Herbert and Dorothy Fields pitched the idea in one sentence to Rodgers & Hammerstein: Ethel Merman as real-life show-woman Annie Oakley. They thought it was a great idea for a show, but thought that they weren't the right writers. Dorothy Fields was to be lyricist and Jerome Kern the composer, but he suddenly died. Berlin was approached, and at first declined, as he didn't feel comfortable writing a complete score for the then new style of integrated musicals. He was persuaded to give it a try, and came back a few days later with a few songs. The result was a hit-rich score and a huge success for all involved. Berlin's theatre career was completely revitalized. The story takes place in the early years of the 20th century. Annie Oakley is an illiterate hillbilly living near Cincinnati. She demonstrates her remarkable marksmanship with a gun, and is persuaded to join Buffalo Bill's traveling Wild West Show. She and Frank fall in love (she lets him win a shooting contest so she can win him). Annie is a brash and sunny character, and "I Got the Sun in the Morning" shows that about her, a song she sings after she's agreed to sell all her golden trophies and jewels in order to finance a merger of Buffalo Bill's show with Pawnee Bill's show. A movie adaptation was released in 1950.

ANYONE CAN WHISTLE
Opened on Broadway: 4/4/64
Music & Lyrics: Stephen Sondheim
Book: Arthur Laurents
Director: Arthur Laurents
Choreographer: Herbert Ross

Something of a "cult" musical (it only played 9 performances on Broadway), *Anyone Can Whistle* is an allegorical satire about a corrupt mayor of a bankrupt town who comes up with a scheme to attract tourists: a fake miracle in which a stream of water appears to spout out a solid rock. The town soon becomes a Mecca for the gullible and the pious, but the hoax is exposed when the inmates of the local mental institution (it's called the Cookie Jar) get mixed up with the pilgrims. Fay is the head nurse at the Cookie Jar. She's so uptight and inhibited that she can't whistle, or express love or emotion of any kind except vague neurosis. The show was a flop, but the Sondheim loyalists have kept it alive. The title song has become a theatre standard.

BABES IN ARMS
Opened on Broadway: 4/14/37
Music: Richard Rodgers
Lyrics: Lorenz Hart
Book: Richard Rodgers & Lorenz Hart
Director: Robert Sinclair
Choreographer: George Balanchine

Babes in Arms boasted more hits than any other Rodgers and Hart musical. Like many musicals of the '20s and '30s, the plot is very light, intended to serve as a loose structure for musical numbers. In the high-spirited, youthful show, a group of teenagers, whose parents are out-of-work vaudevillians, stage a revue to keep from being sent to a work farm. Unfortunately, the show is a bomb. Later, when a transatlantic French flyer lands nearby, they are able to attract enough publicity to put on a successful show and build their own youth center. In 1959 the plot of the show was revised for a New York revival, the characters' names were changed, and the song list slightly altered. (There was never much of a plot anyway.) The 1939 movie version featured Judy Garland and Mickey Rooney. "I Wish I Were in Love Again" shows the characteristic lively wit of lyricist Lorenz Hart.

GOOD NEWS

Opened on Broadway: 9/6/27
Music: Ray Henderson
Lyrics: B.G. DeSylva & Lew Brown
Book: Laurence Schwab & B.G. DeSylva
Director: Edgar MacGregor
Choreographer: Bobby Connolly

Good News inaugurated a series of bright and breezy DeSylva, Brown & Henderson musical comedies that captured the fast-paced spirit of America's flaming youth of the 1920s. In this collegiate caper (and collegiate capers were in vogue then), the setting is Tait College, where the student body is composed of flappers and sheiks. The biggest issue is whether the school's football hero will be allowed to play in the big game against Colton, despite his failing grade in astronomy. He gets a tutor and makes the grade, plays the game and falls in love. It's all very light and good-natured silliness. "I Want to Be Bad" is the big flapper number in the show. MGM released a movie version in 1947. Trying to ride on the nostalgia wave of the 1970s, the show was unsuccessfully revived on Broadway in 1974.

GYPSY

Opened on Broadway: 5/21/59
Music: Jule Styne
Lyrics: Stephen Sondheim
Book: Arthur Laurents
Director-Choreographer: Jerome Robbins

Written for Ethel Merman, who gave the performance of her career as Gypsy Rose Lee's domineering mother, *Gypsy* is one of the great scores in the mature musical comedy tradition. The musical is based on Gypsy Rose Lee's autobiography. Originally Stephen Sondheim was to have written both music and lyrics, but Merman insisted on the more experienced Jule Styne. In the story, Mama Rose is determined to escape from her humdrum life by pushing the talent of her daughter June. After June runs away to get married, Rose focuses all her attention on her other, less talented daughter, the previously neglected Louise. After a few years Louise turns into celebrated burlesque stripper Gypsy Rose Lee. Early in the play Rose meets Herbie and they are attracted to one another. In a quiet moment together she sings "Small World."
Angela Lansbury played Rose in London and on Broadway in a 1974 production, and Tyne Daley played the role in a Broadway revival of 1989. Bette Midler played role in a film made for television in 1994. Rosalind Russell was in the movie version released in 1962.

KISS ME, KATE

Opened on Broadway: 12/30/48
Music & Lyrics: Cole Porter
Book: Samuel & Bella Spewack
Director: John C. Wilson
Choreographer: Hanya Holm

At a time when Broadway thought that Cole Porter was all but washed up after years of mediocre shows, here came *Kiss Me, Kate* to prove that he was still in top form. *Kiss Me, Kate* tells the backstage story of a theatre company in a pre-Broadway tour at Ford's Theatre in Baltimore with a musical version of Shakespeare's *The Taming of the Shrew*. The scenes alternately take place in the actual show-within-a-show and backstage. The stars of the Shakespeare musical are Fred Graham and his ex-wife Lilli Vanessi, still at each other's throats in post divorce anger (note the Shakespeare plot parallels), and the other "couple" from the company's cast, Bill Calhoun and his girlfriend Lois Lane (yes, that's actually her name and it has nothing to do with a man in tights and a cape). Lois is a bit of a goodtime girl, out to have fun, but she apparently does have sincere feelings for Bill. He's a gambler and a two-timer. Lois clearly has her own ideas about relationships, as she reveals in "Always True to You in My Fashion." The 1953 movie version (*Kiss Me Kate*—without the comma in Hollywood), starring Kathryn Grayson, Howard Keel and Ann Miller, was actually filmed in 3-D, another short-lived movie industry experiment to get people away from TV.

LES MISÉRABLES

Opened in Paris: 9/80; **Opened in London:** 10/8/85; **Opened on Broadway:** 3/12/87
Music: Claude-Michel Schönberg
Lyrics: Herbert Kretzmer, original French text by Alain Boublil & Jean-Marc Natel;
additional material by James Fenton
Directors: Trevor Nunn & John Caird

The pop opera, set in France of the 1820s and 1830s, is based on the novel by nineteenth century French novelist Victor Hugo. After a complex exposition, Jean Valjean becomes a factory owner and rises to the position of mayor of Montreuil-sur-mer. One of the workers in his factory, Fantine, has an illegitimate child. She is scorned by her co-workers and turns to the streets to support herself and her daughter, Cosette. After Fantine's death the girl was housed for five years at an inn by abusive foster parents, the Thrénadiers. Their natural daughter was Eponine. Jean Valjean Cosette takes her to Paris with him. Nine years later, in 1832, the scene is Paris. The Thrénadiers are now running a street gang there. The street urchin Eponine is secretly in love with the student Marius. He's in love with Cosette. The waifish Eponine reluctantly agrees to help him find her. There is a student revolt in progress in Paris. Eponine joins the insurrection. She is completely and fully in love with Marius, though it remains her secret, and she sings "On My Own." Eponine is later killed in battle.

ON A CLEAR DAY YOU CAN SEE FOREVER

Opened on Broadway: 10/17/65
Music: Burton Lane
Lyrics & Book: Alan Jay Lerner
Director: Robert Lewis
Choreographer: Herbert Ross

Alan Jay Lerner's fascination with the phenomenon of extrasensory perception led to his teaming with composer Richard Rodgers in 1962 to write a musical called *I Picked a Daisy*. Due to personality conflicts the collaboration was short-lived. Lerner then turned to Burton Lane. Their musical, now called *On a Clear Day You Can See Forever*, is about Daisy Gamble, an unusual woman who can not only predict the future, but when hypnotized by analyst Dr. Mark Bruckner (Daisy went for hypnosis to quit smoking) she is able to recall her past life as Melinda Wells in 18th century London. Mark becomes infatuated with Melinda, making her something of a rival to the real-life Daisy. She falls in love with Mark. Both characters sing the song "He Wasn't You" (or "She Wasn't You") about each other. Barbara Harris played Daisy on Broadway. The 1970 film version starred Barbra Streisand. The show was revived Off-Broadway in the 1990s.

ON YOUR TOES

Opened on Broadway: 4/11/36
Music: Richard Rodgers
Lyrics: Lorenz Hart
Book: George Abbott, Richard Rodgers, Lorenz Hart
Director: Worthington Miner (George Abbott, uncredited)
Choreographer: George Balanchine

On Your Toes was the first musical comedy to combine that genre with ballet. The story is of how Junior Dolan, an ex-vaudevillian who is now a music teacher in New York, persuades a classical ballet company to perform a modern work entitled "Slaughter on Tenth Avenue." He assumes the leading male role himself in the production. Junior is smitten with the prima ballerina, Vera, which makes her lover so irate that he hires two thugs to kill Junior right on stage. He manages to dodge them until the police arrive. The production marked the Broadway debut of choreographer George Balanchine. The musical was revived on Broadway in 1954 and 1983. A film version of the show was released in 1939.

PETER PAN

Opened on Broadway: 10/20/54
Music: Mark Charlap; additional music by Jule Styne
Lyrics: Carolyn Leigh; additional lyrics by Betty Comden & Adolph Green
Book: based on the play by James M. Barrie
Director-Choreographer: Jerome Robbins

This version of *Peter Pan* was originally conceived as a play with a few added songs by Charlap and Leigh. As the concept evolved it was turned into a full-fledged musical and Styne and Comden and Green were brought in to write the rest of the score. Mary Martin was Peter (in a "pants role" as the magical boy character) in this 1954 production. Though the show only ran 152 performances on Broadway, it was telecast many times, making this the version of Peter Pan most people recognize. But it was by no means the only one. Barrie's original play was first produced in New York in 1905. In 1924 stage star Marilyn Miller starred as Peter, with added songs by Jerome Kern. In 1950 Jean Arthur played Peter, with Boris Karloff as Hook, with five songs by Leonard Bernstein. In 1979 a revival of the 1954 musical played on Broadway featuring Sandy Duncan as Peter. "Never Never Land" is Peter's enticing description of the magical fantasy place of dreams.

SIMPLE SIMON

Opened on Broadway: 2/18/30
Music: Richard Rodgers
Lyrics: Lorenz Hart
Book: Ed Wynn & Guy Bolton
Director: Zeke Colvan
Choreographer: Seymour Felix

This Ziegfeld production starred Ed Wynn who played Sion, a fellow who runs a newsstand in Coney Island. He spends his time dreaming of fairy tales like Cinderella. There was a plot about a good kingdom and an evil kingdom. Like most musical comedies of the time the plot was just a light structure that served as a framework for musical numbers. "Ten Cents a Dance" was written for Ruth Etting, who by all accounts performed it in her special tough little girl style. The song really has no plot context in the script. She just comes on and sings it. It stands alone as a scene unto itself very well anyway. A famous performance of this standard was given by Doris Day, playing Ruth Etting, in the 1955 film *Love Me or Leave Me*.

Always True to You in My Fashion

from KISS ME, KATE

Words and Music by
COLE PORTER

slave? I'm just mad for you, And I'll al - ways be, But nat - ur - al - ly,

dolce rit. Suddenly hot

If a cus - tom tail - ored vet___ Asks me out for some - thing wet,___
asked to have a meal___ By a big ty - coon in steel,___

When the vet be - gins to pet,___ I cry "hoo - ray!"___
If the meal in - cludes a deal,___ ac - cept I may!

But I'm al - ways true to you,___ dar - lin', in my fash - ion,

Yes, I'm al-ways true to you,___ dar-lin' in my way.___

I en-joy a ten-der pass___ By the boss of Bos-ton
I could nev-er curl my lip___ To a dazz-lin' dia-mond

Mass. Though his pass is mid-dle class___ and not "Back Bay!"___
clip, Though the clip meant "let 'er rip"___ I'd not say "Nay!"___

But I'm al-ways true to you,___ dar-lin' in my fash-ion.

Yes, I'm al-ways true to you,— dar-lin', in my way.—

There's a mad-man known as "Mack"— Who is
There's an oil man known as "Tex" — Who is

plan-ning to at-tack, — If his mad at-tack— means a Cad-il-lac,— O-
keen to give me checks— And his checks I fear,— mean that Tex is here— to

kay!
stay!

But I'm al-ways true to you,— dar-lin', in my

Glad to Be Unhappy
from ON YOUR TOES

Words by LORENZ HART
Music by RICHARD RODGERS

here I am, More than glad to be un-hap-py.

Un-re-qui-ted love's a bore, And I've got it pret-ty

bad. But for some-one you a-dore,

It's a pleas-ure to be sad. Like a stray-ing

ba - by lamb   With no mam-my and no pap - py,_____ I'm so un -

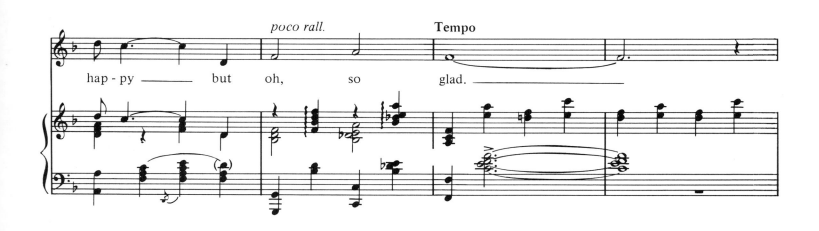

hap - py _____ but oh, so glad. _____

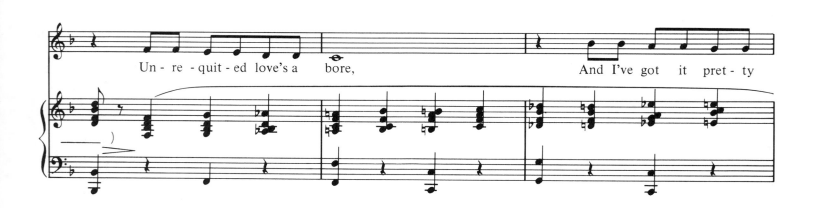

Un - re - quit - ed love's a bore,   And I've got it pret - ty

I Want to Be Bad
from GOOD NEWS

Words and Music by B.G. DeSYLVA,
LEW BROWN and RAY HENDERSON

Good or bad which is the best for me?

marc.

When you're af-ter fun and laugh-ter This ag-gra-vates__ you

8vb

Some re-form-er says a warm-er cli-mate a-waits__ you.

8vb

Refrain

If it's naugh-ty to rouge your lips _ Shake your shoul-ders and twist your hips _

p − f rhythmic

Let a la-dy con-fess I want to be bad _____

If it's naught-y to vamp the men ___ Sleep each morn-ing till af-ter ten ___

Then the an-swer is "yes, I want to be bad." _____ This thing of

be-ing a good lit-tle "Good-ie" is all ver-y well. _____

marcato
cresc.

Anyone Can Whistle

from ANYONE CAN WHISTLE

Words and Music by
STEPHEN SONDHEIM

some - one tell me why can't I? L. H. rit.

I can dance a tan-go, I can read Greek -- Eas-y. *a tempo*

I can slay a dra-gon an-y old week -- Eas-y. _____ What's

hard is sim - ple. What's nat-u-ral comes hard. rit.

May-be you could show me how to let go, low-er my guard,

learn to be free, May-be if you whis-tle, whis - tle for me.

I Got the Sun in the Morning

from the Stage Production ANNIE GET YOUR GUN

Words and Music by
IRVING BERLIN

Small World
from GYPSY

Words by STEPHEN SONDHEIM
Music by JULE STYNE

Rath-er than set-tling down.__ Fun - ny, ____ 'Cause I love to go trav -'ling__

Small world, Is-n't it? We have so much in com-mon,

It's a phe-nom-e - non. We could pool our re-sourc-es

By join-ing forc-es from now on.__ Luck-y, You're a man who likes chil-dren,

I Wish I Were in Love Again

from BABES IN ARMS

Words by LORENZ HART
Music by RICHARD RODGERS

This is a duet in the show.

love-ly lov-ing and the hate-ful hates, The con - ver - sa - tion with the fly - ing plates, I

wish I were in love a-gain! No__ more pain, No__ more

strain, Now__ I'm sane but __ I would rath-er be ga - ga!__ The

pulled out fur of cat and cur, The fine mis - mat-ing of a him and her, I've

learned my les - son, but I wish I were in love a - gain.

With freedom

ad lib.

You don't know that I felt good__ when we up and part - ed.__ You don't know I

knocked on wood,__ glad - ly bro - ken heart - ed.__ Wor - ry - ing is through, I sleep all night__

Ap - pe - tite and health re - stored. You don't know how much I'm bored!

a tempo

The fur-tive sigh, The black-ened eye, The words "I'll love you till the day I die," The self de-cep-tion that be-lieves the lie, I wish I were in love a-gain! When love con-geals it soon re-veals the faint a-ro-ma of per-form-ing seals, The dou-ble cross-ing of a pair of heels, I wish I were in

love a-gain! No_ more care, No_ des - pair,

I'm _ all there now, _ But I'd rath - er be punch drunk! _ Be-

lieve me, sir, I much pre - fer the clas - sic bat - tle of a him and her, I

don't like qui - et and I wish I were in love a - gain!

He Wasn't You

from ON A CLEAR DAY YOU CAN SEE FOREVER

Lyrics by ALAN JAY LERNER
Music by BURTON LANE

What could I do? He was-n't you.

rubato

He was-n't you and no vows ev-er chained me. No,

he was-n't you and good-byes nev-er pained me.

poco rall.

Now I know Why ev-'ry hope al-ways fad-ed so

fast: _____

On - ly with you was I born to live;

On - ly to you have I love to give, Love that for all of a life - time will

rall.

last.

p

rit.

On My Own

from LES MISÉRABLES

Music by CLAUDE-MICHEL SCHÖNBERG
Lyrics by ALAIN BOUBLIL, HERBERT KRETZMER,
JOHN CAIRD, TREVOR NUNN and JEAN-MARC NATEL

EPONINE:

And now I'm all a-lone a-gain, no-where to go, no one to turn to.

I did not want your mon-ey sir, I came out here 'cos I was told to, And now the night is

near, Now I can make be - lieve he's here.

Some-times I walk a-lone at night when ev-ery-bod-y else is sleep - ing,

I think of him and then I'm hap-py with the com-pa-ny I'm keep - ing. The ci - ty goes to

rall. **Andante**

bed And I can live in - side my head.

On my own, pre - tend - ing he's be -
rain, the pave - ment shines like

side me, All a - lone I walk with him 'til
sil - ver, All the lights are mis - ty in the

morn - ing. With - out him I feel his arms a -
riv - er. In the dark - ness, the trees are full of

44

Ten Cents a Dance
from SIMPLE SIMON

Words by LORENZ HART
Music by RICHARD RODGERS

Never Never Land
from PETER PAN

Lyric by BETTY COMDEN and ADOLPH GREEN
Music by JULE STYNE

once you have found your way there, __ You can nev - er nev - er grow old.

So come with me where dreams are born, and time is nev - er planned.

8va

Just think of love-ly things, and your heart will fly on wings for - ev - er __ in

Nev - er, Nev - er Land. _____

ff

rall.